EUROPA  MILITARIA N°33

Modern British
WEBBING EQUIPMENT

SIMON HOWLETT

THE CROWOOD PRESS

First published in 2009 by
The Crowood Press Ltd
Ramsbury, Marlborough
Wiltshire SN8 2HR

www.crowood.com

British Library Cataloguing-in-Publication Data
A catalogue record for this book is available from the British Library.

ISBN 978 1 84797 140 1

Designed and typeset by Focus Publishing, Sevenoaks, Kent
Printed and bound in Malaysia by Times Offset (M) Sdn Bhd

Author's Note

My objective for this book has been to provide a simple overview or reference guide to Modern British Webbing Equipment. Written with collectors and enthusiasts in mind, it starts with the 1958 pattern equipment that served troops for over thirty years, continues with PLCE in some detail, and finally, the latest modular webbing systems and combat body armour issued in Iraq and Afghanistan.

The development of webbing equipment during this time – a period of over half a century – has been vast in both quantity and dimension to say the least; therefore I have remained faithful to the key concepts (for example PLCE) rather than attempting to detail every item ever issued, which would be near impossible! Interesting ancillary and experimental equipment variants are included or referenced for information.

Modern commercial webbing (PLCE) items were often encountered during my research; although these are referenced to where appropriate, they are not individually investigated in great detail as emphasis is quite rightly retained on issued service items.

With all but a few minor exceptions of later dated items or examples, I have endeavoured to feature original equipment items from the periods depicted, these being sourced from personal collections. Some items, particularly experimental parts, are rare, therefore unavailable to photograph (or inaccessible without considerable expenditure) so these are described to the best of my ability.

To enable photography and provide protection for scarce equipment, there are some necessary adjustments to kit layouts and only partial assembly of webbing where required –due care that I am certain fellow collectors will appreciate.

At the back of the book, information on related military publications/ museums and links to websites can be located, so that readers can expand their knowledge, personal collections, or simply browse as desired.

A sincere thank you is due to the following people who have supported this publication: my wife and son for their encouragement; John Ambler (photographic archives manager) at the Royal Marines Museum in Portsmouth for allowing me access to archive material; the Mod DIPR team for images; several re-enactors for allowing me photographic access

to their kit displays; the team at The Crowood Press for their ongoing support; all the team at Sabre Sales in Portsmouth; fellow authors Richard Ingram and Johny Morris for inspiring me to write; John Bodsworth for discussions on military equipment and the 1958/ 1972 pattern nylon experimental equipment images; and finally to my father, Brian Harvey Howlett, for his assistance in editing my manuscript and providing support throughout my latest project.

This book is dedicated to all members of the armed services, past and present, to whom we owe our freedom.

Photography/ Images

A special thanks is due to David Amey for the extensive photographic sessions and kit illustrations used throughout the book. Where stated, the MoD images used within this book are Crown Copyright/MoD, reproduced with the permission of the Controller of Her Majesty's Stationery Office.

Please note that to respect the privacy of individuals (and their families) involved in recent conflicts, the author has used archive photographic material that complies with recently issued censorship guidelines; therefore identities have been erased from all privately sourced photographs. In the case of approved Crown Copyright material, pictures have been selected from stock archive photographs where the subjects' faces are hidden or are not looking at the camera.

About the Author

Simon Howlett has been researching and collecting British webbing equipment for over twenty years. The gift of a basic 1944 pattern set for cadet use started his journey into collecting militaria, and this has evolved into a significant hobby to date. His other interests include researching military small arms as well as cycling and swimming. He lives in Hampshire with his wife and young son.

Simon's established interest in the 1944 pattern equipment led him in 2007 to write his first publication, *British Post-War Jungle Webbing*, which is also available from The Crowood Press (ref: Europa Militaria No. 34). This book explores the webbing and equipment used throughout the 1950s/ 1960s British jungle conflicts.

Contents

List of Abbreviations

ALICE	All-Purpose Load-Carrying Equipment (US webbing)
BFA	Blank Firing Attachment
CEFO	Combat Equipment Fighting Order
CEMO	Combat Equipment Marching Order
CQC	Chelsea Quilt Company
DPM	Disruptive Pattern Material (camouflage)
EOD	Explosive Ordnance Disposal
FIBUA	Fighting In Built-Up Areas
GPMG	General-Purpose Machine Gun
GS	General Service
IRR	Infra-Red Resistant
ITW	Illinois Tool Works (Military Products – Nexus and Fastex)
LCTV	Load-Carrying Tactical Vest
LMG	Light Machine Gun
LTD	Lift the Dot (fastener)
MoD	Ministry of Defence
MOLLE	Modular Lightweight Load-Carrying Equipment
NATO	North Atlantic Treaty Organization
NBC	Nuclear Biological and Chemical
NSN	NATO Stock Number
PALS	Pouch Attachment Ladder System
PCL	Pack Combat Light
PECOC	Personal Equipment and Common Operational Clothing
PLCE	Personal Load-Carrying Equipment
PRR	Personal Role Radio
QR	Quick-Release
RAF	Royal Air Force
RG	Radway Green
SA80	Small Arms 80 (weapons system)
SAS	Special Air Service
SBS	Special Boat Squadron
SLR	Self-Loading Rifle
SMG	Sub Machine Gun
SOP	Standard Operating Procedure(s)
SUIT	Sight Unit Infantry Trilux
SUSAT	Sight Unit Small Arms Trilux
UBAS	Under-Body Armour Shirt
UGL	Underslung Grenade Launcher
WW2	World War Two

Research, Storage and Collector's Guide

Although I have been researching and collecting British webbing equipment for some time, it is always an exciting part of the hobby to discover new equipment or to uncover fresh research information that challenges my thinking on previously understood concepts. Consequently I would welcome any feedback.

In my first book, *British Post-War Jungle Webbing*, I included a basic guide for collectors and researchers, as understanding the surplus market and getting started into militaria are perhaps the most difficult elements. In this publication I have emphasized some of the common advice but refined it towards the collector of modern British equipments. The following notes are from my direct experience (not a dealer's or any commercial perspective) and can be adjusted by the reader accordingly.

In addition within my research, I have found that investigating the associated accoutrements, such as small arms or personal kit, has assisted me greatly in understanding some concepts of webbing design. Throughout this book, topics such as the small arms 80 (SA80) rifle development and nuclear biological and chemical (NBC) protection equipment feature largely for this reason.

Getting Started

During the last few years, interest in militaria has grown considerably, potentially driven by the number of books on the subject; however, this is more likely from the audio-visual and technology advances available to the media, as compared to fifty or even twenty-five years ago. From the number of militaria enthusiasts attending fairs and displays over the years, it is apparent that all types of military kit have become very popular with collectors, and that to meet this demand, the number of professional dealers has subsequently increased. The interest has certainly affected the market and has made it harder to find examples of older equipment at reasonable cost.

In reality, there is actually a wide range of items out there – my advice is that today's militaria enthusiast needs to be patient and selective, and ideally to focus on what they want to collect first and foremost. If you do decide that you want to start collecting webbing, the most important advice for the absolute beginner is not to rush in. Do take your time: read, research and browse kit for a while, and be certain what you want to collect before you dive into trying to 'collect the world'.

Concentrating on a specific historical period or webbing equipment pattern (set) is often the best way forwards. Start your collection with some small items until you gain in confidence and have a full understanding of what you are looking for, and can gauge general prices fairly accurately. As and when the good examples surface, these can be considered in due course according to your budget.

There will always be one item or part of a set that is difficult to find, so do shop around. I find that often (especially on the internet) what one dealer labels as a 'rare' or 'scarce' item, another militaria outlet may have lots available and be happy to sell one at a bargain price just to clear out the stock.

So where is the best 'place' to look for equipment? The more popular locations for finding webbing kit are regular organized militaria fairs, ex-army surplus stores across the UK, and increasingly, internet auction sites. Militaria can even make a surprise appearance at car boot sales, local charity shops and church hall fairs as people clear out their lofts and garages for more room.

(Right) The development of British webbing equipment during the last fifty years has been vast. New collectors are advised to start with a certain militaria theme or a particular set of webbing equipment.

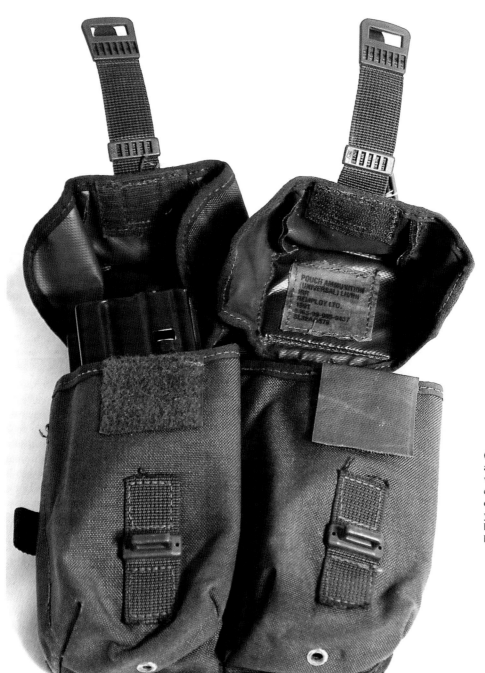

(Left) Olive drab PLCE Universal ammunition pouch shown open, with an SA80 magazine in the left compartment. These early versions of PLCE were only issued for a few years and are worth collecting because in time they are likely to become scarce.

Some people dislike the jumble sale nature of militaria fairs but I really enjoy a good rummage through a pile of kit, finding it quite therapeutic. If every item you wanted was easy to find or available via a tidy shop shelf ('virtual' or otherwise), half the interest (for me, and I suspect others) would be taken away. I have found some fantastic items for 50p in a heap at an annual fair – indeed some items feature in this book!

Collecting must be viewed as a long-term enjoyable hobby. Rewards are reaped over time, so patience is indeed a virtue. Be warned though, this can be addictive!

Within the further reference section at the rear of the book, I have recommended other books, reference material and information sources to assist any new or seasoned collector of British webbing equipment.

Re-enactment Groups

Historical re-enactment is another area growing in popularity, with new living history groups emerging all the time. Many of the re-enactments are based on actual military units featuring in WW2, but interest in more recent conflicts, such as the Gulf War and even those of foreign armies, is now emerging. Some groups include restored military vehicles, which is an amazing hobby in

1958 Pattern Webbing Equipment

The Falklands conflict was the turning point for the British Army's 1958 pattern equipment. Serious shortcomings with the cotton-based webbing were highlighted during the campaign.

The design was twenty-four years old in 1982 and the South Atlantic environment was unlike any other, with the equipment experiencing daily exposure to extreme weather conditions – rain, snow, ice and high winds were typical. But the fact remained that the issue 1958 pattern webbing, whilst robust in construction, had some major disadvantages in that it soaked up rainwater and was very difficult to dry out, leading to shrinking and rot damage. The sub-zero freezing conditions made the wet webbing stiff (it actually froze solid according to some troop reports), adding to the wearer's discomfort. To show the scale of the water-absorption problem, it has been proven from independent service tests carried out that wet 1958 pattern cotton webbing will absorb five times (about 40 per cent) more water than a nylon-based equivalent.

If 1958 pattern webbing could retain large amounts of water, it would in theory be hard to decontaminate in any future conflict where nuclear, biological or chemical (NBC) agents were deployed. Ideally, prevention from agent absorption would be better than removal, because once absorbed into the cotton material it could carry on contaminating the user (and everyone else in the same locality) until fully eradicated.

This fundamental issue led to the demise of the 1958 pattern equipment, although it is a testament to its credibility that it survived until around 1988, before the webbing would be fully withdrawn from front-line service. There is photographic evidence that 1958 pattern equipment was still issued to rear echelon and Territorial Army troops within the first Gulf war, indicating that the changeover to nylon PLCE was still being undertaken even at that time.

Also studied were the various civilian rucksacks acquired by troops within the Falklands *in lieu* of the 1958 pattern large pack. The large pack had long been abandoned as a serious means of transporting equipment due to its low capacity and awkward attachment method on to the set.

The loss of the *Atlantic Conveyor* with several Chinook transport helicopters on board meant that subsequently troops had to walk across the islands into battle, carrying loads sometimes in excess of their own bodyweights. To achieve their load-carrying requirements, soldiers ditched the 1958 pattern large pack and turned to large-capacity rucksacks (or Bergens), such as the Berghaus Cyclops Roc, the SAS/Para Bergen or the 'H'-frame rucksacks, loading them to the hilt. Wearing such a long-backed rucksack with 1958 pattern belt kit required some modification to the basic webbing set, with removal of the kidney pouches being common. This necessity (or practice) was another heavily criticized aspect of the 1958 pattern webbing during the subsequent equipment review.

For the future, a weather-resistant equipment set would also require a large, high-capacity rucksack and one that was compatible with the belt pouches. It is no surprise, therefore, that the subsequent 1980s trials webbing and rucksack is based on these hard-learned principles.

The equipment would also need to accommodate the ongoing 5.56mm (0.223) SA80 weapons system that was being trialled and developed to replace the L2A3 Sterling (9mm/ 0.38) sub machine gun, L1A1 self-loading rifle (7.62mm/ 0.300), and L7 series general purpose machine gun (GPMG) (7.62mm/ 0.300) weapons then in service.

(Left) The Falklands 1982. Two Royal Marines guard a defensive position armed with a GPMG (general-purpose machine gun) and camouflaged SLRs (self-loading rifles). The left-hand man is wearing 1958 pattern webbing equipment. Note the 58 pattern plastic mug at the rear of the trench, illumination flares at hand, and 'Snoopy' attached to the GPMG barrel! (© Crown Copyright/MoD and Trustees of the Royal Marines Museum)

(**Above**) The Falklands, 1982: two Royal Marines march past a Royal Navy Wessex helicopter. The loss of transport helicopters early in the conflict left troops carrying large loads into battle; the man on the right clearly demonstrates this, with what appears to be an ammunition box strapped to a general service (GS) rucksack. Rucksack capacity and design was seriously reviewed after the conflict. (© Crown Copyright/MoD and Trustees of the Royal Marines Museum)

(**Right**) The 1958 pattern large pack, dated 1983. The capacity of the large pack was limited and the item was only used in training in order for recruits to appreciate the value of a quality rucksack. Apart from the limited capacity, the other main fault was trying to remove the pack quickly, because although it could be attached securely with four clips, these proved awkward to detach under pressure. Note the external side pockets and cross-straps for fixing a helmet. The clips that engage D-rings on the yoke and ammunition pouches can be seen on the top and lower side straps.

9

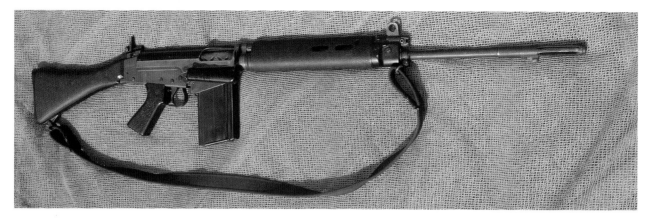

(Above) The 7.62mm L1A1 self-loading rifle. This rifle design was used by both British and Argentinian troops in the Falklands. Feed was from a 20-round magazine.

(Below left) 1958 pattern left-hand ammunition pouches, rear view: (left) early or first pattern with vertical belt 'C' clips; (right) later pattern pouch with angled 'C' clips.

(Below) 1958 first pattern equipment. The second pattern equipment was revised to include yoke attachments to the kidney pouches, pack retention straps on the yoke, and a strap and buckle fastener

on the water bottle (replacing the twist version as shown); the green water bottle was produced in black, and the ammunition pouches were increased in size and produced without the internal munitions strap.

Background and Overview

The 1958 pattern equipment was introduced in about 1960 following extensive troop trials, and was employed in a number of theatres. It was an improvement over the 1937 and 1944 pattern sets, borne out by a subsequent and extensive service life of over thirty years.

Manufactured from dark green dyed woven cotton, the main set consisted of a waist belt, left/ right ammunition pouches, a yoke, a pair of kidney pouches, a poncho roll, a water bottle cover, and finally a large pack.

The initial equipment set (often called 'first pattern') was modified following field use in about 1965 to include larger ammunition pouches, pack retention straps added to the yoke, and upper (yoke) fixings added to the kidney pouches. Some manufacturing adaptations can also be found; for example, kidney pouches were produced with and without metal cover reinforcement strips. All the straps were upgraded, being supplied with more robust end protection tabs. A full explanation of these early

'first issue' variants and history can be found in *British Post-War Jungle Webbing* (EM34), also published by The Crowood Press.

At the time of the Falklands war, 1958 pattern was being heavily modified by soldiers to accommodate the increase in ammunition and to suit the role at hand. The main seven items from the set (excluding the large pack) remained in service throughout its life; however, unofficial adaptations to accommodate increasing personal loads continued to occur out of necessity.

Supplementary items within the set included a Browning 9mm pistol holster, two short utility straps, a padded compass pouch and a padded binocular pouch. Miscellaneous pouches and sleeves for support weapons were also manufactured from the same material. The metalwork was steel, and finished initially in light anodized green; later on, fittings were coloured dark green or black.

(Above) Ancillary items; SLR butt/ support pouch, utility straps (early and late designs), Sight Unit Infantry Trilux (SUIT) pouch, compass case and binocular case. Note the twist fasteners on the cases.

(Below) Combat Equipment Fighting Order (CEFO) – 1958 pattern. This is a typical representation of CEFO during the 1980s.

11

Small Arms 80 Development

Adoption of the SA80: L85A1 and L86A1

During the 1960s to the 1970s the British Army had a number of different calibre weapons in service to suit different tasks, all with various short- and long-range performance characteristics. After considering modern warfare requirements, it was decided in about 1980 to adopt an 'intermediate' range assault weapon (300 to 400m main range) with a semi-automatic and an automatic fire capability.

The British Army had used the AR15/ M16 rifle during the Falklands conflict, and although it was reported to lack range, this was mainly due to a lighter load of 5.56mm ammunition (M193). At one point the AR15 was deemed a favoured replacement for the 7.62mm SLR rifle following interest in smaller calibre weapons. Other forerunners included the 'bullpup' Enfield EM2 system, and the 4.85mm individual weapon (IW) rifles. Both are

(Above) The 5.56mm (0.223) L86A1 light support weapon (LSW) is based on the SA80 rifle and uses 80 per cent of the same components. Designed for the light machine gun (LMG) role, it has a longer barrel than the rifle and is fitted with a supporting bipod. This example has a Radway Green (RG) magazine and is without its Small Unit Small Arms Trilux (SUSAT) telescopic sight.

(Right) The SUSAT sight is a 4× magnification telescopic sight that replaces traditional 'iron' sights on the SA80 weapons. The soldier aims the rifle using a target pointer, and can therefore quickly acquire a sight picture. The unit can also be operated within low light conditions, although early examples suffered from misting when exposed to humid or jungle environments.

(Left) The 5.56mm (0.223) L85A1 Enfield SA80 rifle with sling. This rifle replaced the L1A1 self-loading rifle in front-line service and is capable of both semi-automatic (single shot) and fully automatic fire. Note the bullpup design (compare to the SLR illustrated earlier), where the magazine sits behind the pistol grip; this maximizes barrel length in a short rifle.

worthy of note in the pursuit of the new rifle design, and enthusiasts may wish to research these weapons.

The L85A1 and L86A1 weapons from Enfield were finally brought into service during October 1985. The weapons are more commonly or colloquially known as the SA80 (Small Arms 80) and LSW (light support weapon) respectively. Both would have a fundamental effect on new personal equipment design, and hence this is explored in some detail.

The new weapons used a lighter 5.56mm round and a 30-round magazine. The Sterling 9mm (0.38) SMG, the 7.62mm (0.3) SLR and the GPMG were phased out of front line service (around 1990), although some GPMGs were retained for ongoing fire support roles. A single-action version of the new rifle, designated L98A1, was provided for cadet training in 1987. It operated using the same ammunition and 30-round magazines.

The lighter load (M193) ammunition for the original AR15 (M16) was evaluated, and a more potent 5.56mm round (SS109) was developed. Although 5.56mm ammunition is lighter than the 7.62mm round it replaced, the overall performance of the new ammunition was comparable.

The new single-calibre 5.56mm weapons now only required one type of magazine to be in service, and effectively removed the requirement of a webbing ammunition pouch to accommodate a 'range' of different weapon magazines and belted ammunition. The Americans had taken this stance with their ALICE (All-Purpose Load-Carrying Equipment) equipment since 1974, ensuring the pouch was only used for M16 magazines.

The compatibility of the 5.56mm weapon systems was deliberate as it also allowed spare magazines from the SA80 rifleman to be used by the LSW gunner when required. The modern soldier is now trained on both weapons, and if required a rifleman can fire and maintain the light support weapon (LSW), as both operate the same way.

With lighter ammunition and the fully automatic fire capability on both weapons, soldiers soon realized the pressing need to carry more magazines, especially for FIBUA ('fighting in built-up areas'), which consumed a great deal of ammunition.

The SA80 (L85A1) was initially issued to each soldier supplied with eight 30-round magazines (240 rounds in total). The 240 rounds of smaller calibre ammunition was an increase over the

(**Above**)(Left) A 7.62mm (0.300) round used in the SLR. (Right) A 5.56mm (0.223) round used in the SA80. Although less powerful when compared to 7.62mm, the lighter 5.56mm round allowed more ammunition to be carried, and its lower recoil enabled controlled burst fire. All ammunition shown is inert.

(**Above**) The US ALICE M16 (AR-15) triple magazine pouch. From experience gained during Vietnam, the Americans adopted nylon equipment ahead of the UK, quickly realizing its water-/ chemical-repelling qualities. The pouch is deliberately designed for three magazines, and two grenades can be stored in the side pockets; this prevents other equipment being crammed in. Note the plastic closure, which looks similar to the version adopted for British experimental webbing items.

(**Left**) Prior to the introduction of the SA80 weapons system, the British Army had an array of infantry weapons, all using different magazines and ammunition. (Top) Left to right: 7.62mm round, 7.62mm GPMG ammunition, spare belt links, five-round stripper clip for the SLR, SLR front sight protector, two 9mm Parabellum pistol/ sub machine gun (SMG) rounds, SLR charging device, two 5.56mm rounds for comparison, Sterling SMG 34-round magazine, light machine gun (LMG) 30-round magazine, and 20-round SLR magazine. All ammunition shown is inert.

SLR L1A1 allocation (7.62mm x 100 rounds in five magazines) and the 9mm Sterling L2A3 SMG (160 rounds in five magazines).

Incidentally, the Americans, using their M16 (with a similar rate of automatic fire) during Vietnam, found that a more realistic combat load was 400–500 rounds!

Due to the initial unavailability of a MoD manufactured magazine, the compatible and reliable 30-round aluminium M16 magazine was used until Radway Green (RG) produced an aluminium version. The RG magazines (stamped 'RG' on the base follower) were based on the M16 version. Although these did function as designed, the economy of the materials meant the user had to be very careful not to dent or distort the magazine case/ feed-lips, otherwise stoppages would occur – a difficult request for a soldier! Inside the magazine, the feed ramp that supports the ammunition (produced from plastic) was a source of stoppages, because after some use it did not follow exactly parallel with the magazine case and could jam. In addition, rounds would have to be precisely loaded with their bases right up to the rear of the magazine or again, the feed ramp could jam.

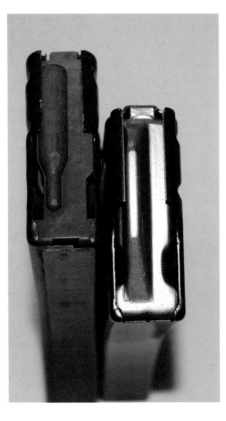

(Far left) Feed-lips of SA80 magazines: (Left) Radway Green with plastic follower; and (right) H&K improved magazine with metal follower plate. The feed-lips were redesigned to prevent stoppages from distortion, a common problem with the early aluminium magazines.

(Left) The plastic charging device fitted to a magazine. To charge the magazine, thumb pressure is applied to the rounds until all are inserted into the magazine. The empty clip strip is then discarded, and the operation repeated until the magazine is full.

Suffice to say, the more reliable M16 magazine soon became a popular 'long term' acquisition amongst soldiers after the SA80 was adopted, as it was superior to the British version. It was rumoured that the new British aluminium magazine was going to be a single use or disposable item, but that rumour appears to have been quashed on economic grounds!

Ammunition was supplied in ten-round stripper clips. To assist the loading of magazines directly from the clips, a plastic speed-loader was produced. This sat on top of the magazine and allowed the rounds held in the stripper clip to be pressed into the magazine using the thumb.

(Below) Ammunition for the SA80 was provided in green nylon five-pocket bandoliers containing 150 rounds. Each pocket contained three 10-round stripper clips (30 rounds), or one magazine of ammunition.

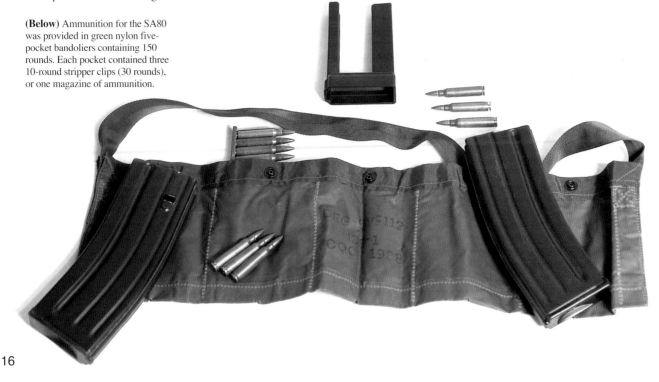

The SA80 A2 (L85A2 & L86A2)

The early SA80 / L85A1 rifles, whilst extremely accurate with their 4× magnification SUSAT optical sights, obtained a reputation for poor mechanical reliability. The issues encountered with the weapon are well documented, but to précis combat reports following usage in the Gulf War (1991) and peace-keeping actions from the early 1990s, initial usage revealed over 100 problems, ranging from the plastic furniture melting in contact with insect repellent to accidental release of the magazine. This clearly prompted an urgent review of these fundamental design issues.

In the late 1990s, Heckler & Koch (H&K), a well known company for producing high quality weapons such as the MP5 SMG, were contracted to revise the L85A1 rifle, and as a consequence, many changes were effected, resulting in the L85A2 and L86A2 LSW emerging into service in about 2002. Externally, the weapons appear the same except for some slight differences, the revised cocking handle on the new rifle being perhaps the most prominent identification feature, for example. One major change was a stronger magazine, which although a heavier replacement than its aluminium predecessor, was without doubt more reliable.

Recent simulated battle-testing of the SA80 A2 weapon system in sandy conditions and combined prolonged fire test (firing over 24,000 rounds) resulted in a 95 per cent success rate with no serious defects; this compares very favourably to other similar weapon systems.

(Above) (Left) Radway Green (RG) magazine; (right) new H&K magazine for the L85A2 SA80. Note the difference in base plate design.

(Below) (Left) Stripped H&K revised SA80 A2 30-round magazine; and (right), an early Radway Green (RG) magazine. The difference in build quality/construction is clear.

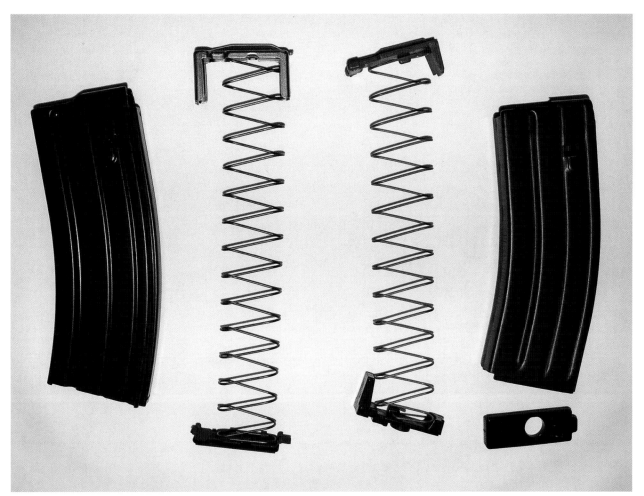

Trial and Experimental Webbing

Introduction

The experience of 1958 pattern in the Falklands conflict confirmed its unsuitability for modern combat. Although a respected load-carrying system, decontamination within a NBC environment was poor. Development of new equipment in nylon, and to improve flexible load carrying, had actually commenced prior to the conflict, but this mostly consisted of Special Forces' requirements and small trials for other specialist units where equipment carriage necessitated a degree of flexibility. This research started during the late 1960s and influenced the design of the original PLCE in due course. In this section I have chosen some elements of experimental equipment to demonstrate how the PLCE design was arrived at.

SAS Vest

During the 1960s, the Special Air Service (SAS) experimented with combat vests and designed a garment suitable for jungle warfare consisting of two front pouches and a larger rear pack. The design was an innovation, and it is still a popular acquisition today. Commonly known as the 'SAS vest', other official references include the 'pack combat light' (or PCL).

(Below) The SAS vest as worn. The vest was adjusted for the user with side straps. Note the four belt straps at the base of the equipment. A normal webbing belt could be inserted to keep the vest in place when fully loaded, or to add extra equipment, for example water bottles. In recent conflicts, the vest was used to store escape and evasion equipment either being worn on, or stored at, the top of a rucksack.

The equipment 'vest' or jerkin is not a new concept. Such a garment was trialled during WW2, but it did not see subsequent widespread issue. The main reported disadvantage of that version was the use of canvas material, which when worn as a jacket made a soldier overheat. This was unfortunate, because the load-carrying capacity was significantly increased compared to 1937 pattern webbing, and offered a greater degree of general comfort.

The SAS vest is made from polyurethane-coated nylon material and consists of a one-piece mesh on which the pouches are mounted. The two large front pouches are closed using two-prong plastic clips, similar to those found on US equipment. These allowed a pouch to be opened and closed with one hand, which was easier than the 1944 pattern cloth quick-release versions. At the front of the ammunition pouches a single magazine 'sleeve' is affixed enabling quick magazine changes if required (at the time, for the SLR). The garment is closed at the front with two toggles. The rear single compartment pouch is closed with nylon tape ties. The garment is adjusted to the user with lateral straps at the sides of the equipment.

At the base of the equipment, four loops are fitted to accommodate a webbing belt that can be attached to ensure the garment sits comfortably under load. This could also provide the facility of extra belt kit if required.

The availability of modern nylon materials and the fact that a strong 'mesh' was used to infill between pouches or provide shoulder straps, did away with the overheating problem encountered with the 'battle jerkin' of 1942.

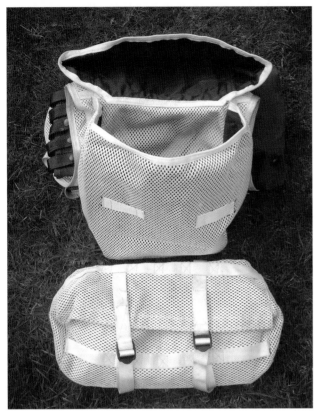

(Above) The rear of the SBS vest, showing the fixed backpack and separate compartment for a sleeping bag.

(Above right) The SBS vest. This is closer to an operational waistcoat in design, but has been left in this section for reference. Note the white mesh, front zip and the green magazine/ ration pouches. Pouch closures are poppers and Velcro.

(Right) The front of the SAS vest. Note the PLCE 'Spanish' clip closures, the quick-grab magazine pouch (on the front), and the toggle closures.

(Below) The inside of the SAS vest. Note the mesh element of the garment, on to which the pouches were attached/ mounted. Being a mesh, it assisted the user to keep cool by allowing heat and perspiration to escape through it.

The pouches of the SAS vest can be customized according to the operation and therefore enable a considerable load to be carried, including large quantities of 7.62mm GPMG belted ammunition – hence the alternative nickname of 'GPMG vest' occasionally bestowed upon this item.

Note that even at this early stage of experimental equipment development, the 1958 pattern equipment pouches were considered too small and restrictive to different weapon loads.

The vest's features are clearly geared to Special Forces' requirements. Originally it was designed with jungle operations in mind, a lightweight waterproof vest with reasonable load capacity. In the 1982 Falklands conflict, the vest served as a popular operational waistcoat to 'top up' webbing belt kit or as a survival pack. Examples of this practice were seen amongst archive pictures, and more recently, equipping the members of Bravo Two Zero, the famous SAS anti-Scud missile patrol from the 1991 Gulf War.

Illustrated is a modern DPM nylon version made by CQC (Chelsea Quilt Company), although there are several examples available to the collector including the original green butyl nylon version, and others exist with Fastex (or side-release) clips provided on the front/ rear pouches.

This DPM version is the same size as the original green nylon vest from the late 1960s, and has 'Spanish' tab closures (so named after their origination) on the front pouches, indicating that it must be a recently manufactured example. The manufacturer's stamp (CQC) – not illustrated – is printed to the rear inside pouch flap.

An experimental item similar to the SAS vest has also been manufactured for the Special Boat Squadron (SBS) and used in the Falklands conflict. This version is manufactured with a white mesh chassis and fitted with olive-coloured ammunition pouches. Separate rear compartments are fitted for equipment/ sleeping bags.

Although the SAS vest design is over forty years old, the concept of mesh and vest construction can still be encountered on a number of military and civilian items, including SAS counter-terrorist equipment, civilian hi-visibility jerkins, rucksacks and police patrol equipment.

1972 Pattern Webbing

The 1972 pattern equipment was an attempt to build a basic waterproof modular webbing rig consisting of large front pouches and a rear rucksack. It appears to have been designed based on the SAS vest layout and nylon material. The equipment is also constructed with coated polyurethane, two-layer nylon material similar in respects to the Mark Two S6 respirator case and GS Bergen. This waterproofed material provides decontamination from NBC material, and is a significant improvement over cotton webbing and the primary purpose for its introduction.

The set comprises two large front pouches (left and right), a yoke and a large back/ rear pouch. The front pouches are larger than 1958 pattern and have a single magazine pouch mounted alongside so that fast magazine changes can be performed without opening the main pouch compartment. The pouch closures are plastic with two prongs (the design is taken from the earlier SAS vest). Stud or popper closures are used on the smaller side magazine pouches, of which there are two settings – high and low. The right-hand pouch has loops to accommodate the SLR bayonet, and the left has two straps/ buckles for attaching other kit. Both pouches have a patch of white material attached to the rear on which to write the owner's name/ number.

The pouches are not mounted on a separate waist belt; instead each pouch has the male/ female elements of an adjustable belt, the left pouch having the male prong/ clip and the right-hand

(**Below**) The front pouches of the 1972 pattern equipment. Larger than 1958 equivalents, each side had a dedicated magazine pocket and part of the waist belt permanently mounted. The straps at the top fix into the yoke buckles.

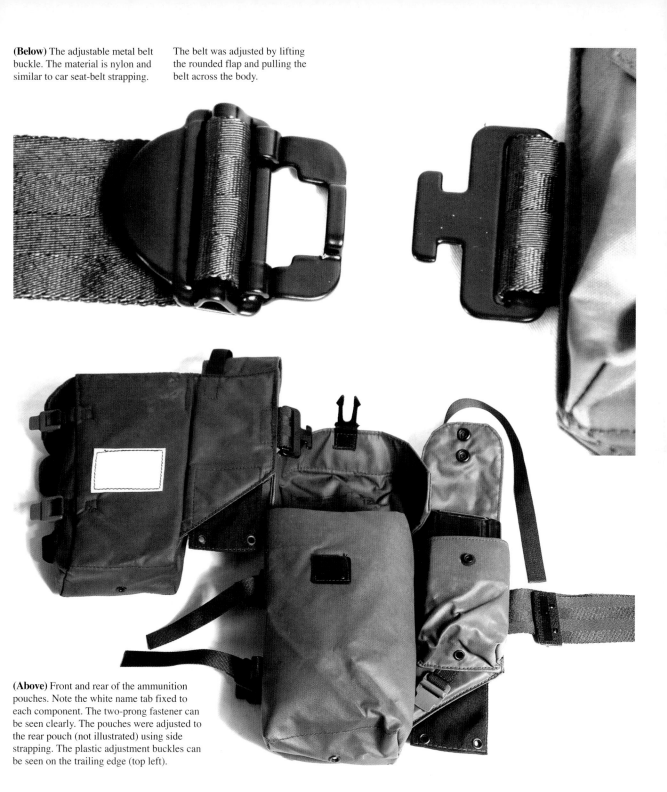

(Below) The adjustable metal belt buckle. The material is nylon and similar to car seat-belt strapping.

The belt was adjusted by lifting the rounded flap and pulling the belt across the body.

(Above) Front and rear of the ammunition pouches. Note the white name tab fixed to each component. The two-prong fastener can be seen clearly. The pouches were adjusted to the rear pouch (not illustrated) using side strapping. The plastic adjustment buckles can be seen on the trailing edge (top left).

side the adjustable buckle and strap. Early patterns of the equipment were fitted with metal side adjustment clips; these were later changed for plastic (as per the illustration).

The rear pouch was one of two designs: with and without a machete carrier. The carrier is positioned at the base of the sack and may indicate an intention for this set to be used in the jungle. The pack was effectively a small, single compartment sack that was closed with a draw cord and two flat straps. The overall capacity was limited, which affected its adoption into wider infantry use. Also illustrated is a larger rucksack (with external frame) made from the same nylon material and using the same 1972 pattern closures – and interestingly, cloth ties that feature on the SAS vest. This developed into the 50ltr (11gal) GS Bergen in due course.

21

(Above) 1972 pattern belt order with front pouches, rear haversack and yoke design. The yoke is clearly influenced from the 1958 pattern. (© John Bodsworth 2009)

(Below) 1972 pattern (GS) Bergen. Note the nylon material, closure ties, external frame and fastener clips. (© John Bodsworth 2009)

(Above right) Early SUIT pouch made from 1972 pattern nylon material. Note the fastener clip. (© John Bodsworth 2009)

The yoke was similar in design to the 1958 pattern version, and connected the pouches at the front using a 1944 pattern double quick-release buckle and to the rear, using two plastic clips unique to this equipment.

On inspection the system appears to initially address the key issue of easing NBC decontamination and flexible provision for weapon ammunition. If any criticism of the set can be made, it appears from trial reports that the equipment fittings were not robust enough and the set came apart. The main issue was the rear pack interfering with the carriage of a large rucksack, which was required given the amount of equipment in service use (and later demonstrated in the Falklands conflict). The 1972 pattern pack would just accommodate the issue NBC suit, over-boots and other material – essentials given its intention.

It is not immediately obvious how other essential items were added into the set. The front pouches both have eyelets for attachment of the 1944 pattern wire hanger – but this is not the ideal place to add a machete case or swinging water bottle (ouch!). The side straps cannot support more pouches easily. This lack of flexibility and fixed pouch layout merely added to its service rejection.

Butyl Nylon Material
The butyl nylon material seen in the experimental items was used to construct a number of issued items and rucksacks, including the GS Bergen, SAS/ Para Bergen (not illustrated), S6 respirator haversack and other ancillary equipment pouches. The nylon material and the items made from it are important to consider in the development of British webbing. The GS Bergen was used in the Falklands, but being of small capacity it was only useful for short patrols. The SAS/ PARA Bergen was developed for protracted Special Forces operations. Its capacity was a huge 120 litres (26.4gal), and its construction was deliberately robust in order to survive the constant battering of parachute insertions. A metal frame (heavy on its own!) was externally attached. To use this rucksack, soldiers would have to adapt their 58 pattern equipment to accommodate the longer frame (usually by removing the kidney pouches). The S6 respirator cases are illustrated later in the book.

Experimental Nylon Webbing, 1958 Pattern

In attempting to make a 'waterproof' webbing set, several concepts were investigated before starting a complete redesign of equipment, including converting 1958 pattern to a nylon set. Firstly the existing cotton 1958 pattern equipment was covered with a nylon fabric, which although initially effective was not robust in the long term, and the few pictures that do exist, show the nylon material ripped and peeling from pouches.

The second, more effective manufacturing method was to construct the pouches from scratch using a robust nylon material, different from the coated polyurethane type of before.

1958 pattern nylon sets were trialled in the 1970s in small num-

bers, and very few full examples of these webbing sets exist today. The components and fundamental design, size and layout of the 1958 pattern nylon variant remained unchanged from the previous cotton set. The metalwork and fittings were also carried over. Collectors are likely to encounter the SUIT (Sight Unit Infantry Trilux) pouch manufactured from a similar material on the surplus market.

The concept appears reasonable. As for the set not being widely issued, the cost, durability and the forthcoming adoption of a new rifle system may have counted against it. All these points appear feasible in the scheme of events. Had the ammunition pouches been redesigned for the new rifle and the kidney pouches lowered, would this nylon set still be in operation?

23

(Right) Close detail of the nylon tab and metalwork. 1958 pattern fixtures were retained from the cotton equipment set.

(Below) The SUIT pouch manufactured from textured nylon material. This fabric was used to produce a trial version of the 1958 pattern equipment.

(Right) Further items from the 1958 pattern nylon set are shown: top: water-bottle carrier and respirator case; bottom: kidney pouches. (© John Bodsworth 2009)

Commercial Nylon Webbing

During the late 1980s the limitations of the cotton-based 1958 pattern webbing brought the development of commercial nylon-based kit on to the external equipment market, as soldiers sought upgrades to their 1958 pattern webbing. Examples of commercial items include nylon versions of kidney pouches, NBC equipment carriers, and ammunition pouches more suited to the new 30-round magazines and drop clip tabs, allowing the lowering of standard ammunition pouches in 'SAS' style.

PLCE Trials Equipment (1985 Pattern PLCE)

The adoption of the SA80 rifle in 1985 also came at a point where the potential of military operations in NBC environments was becoming a real threat. Britain would be drawn into a desert war shortly after the equipment's inauguration, and the likelihood of NBC weapons being used by Iraq was a very clear and present danger.

Throughout the 1980s, several trial versions of load-carrying equipment were tested, and the set developed in 1985–89 would be selected to become 1990 pattern PLCE. Speaking to a fellow collector, it is known that at least four versions were designed and issued for troop trials from 1983 onwards! The illustrated pattern of trial equipment is often called '1985 pattern PLCE', which was the year this particular set was trialled amongst troops and demonstrated at the School of Infantry. Examples of the 1985 trial equipment are shown.

(Right) Basic trial belt order with trial yoke and belt; left to right: ammunition pouches and a utility pouch in the centre.

(Below) Experimental PLCE equipment layout, circa 1985 at Commando Training Centre, Royal Marines (CTCRM). The modular concept of PLCE is clearly seen across these pouches. Top to bottom: utility straps, bungee cords, hip belt, waist belt, utility/water-bottle pouches; (below) ammunition pouches, left to right: main yoke, shovel (on its plastic cover), shovel webbing case, blocks – unknown?, respirator pouch, and far right, side pouch yoke. At the base, the rucksack and side pouches provide a large load-carrying capacity. (© Trustees of the Royal Marines Museum)

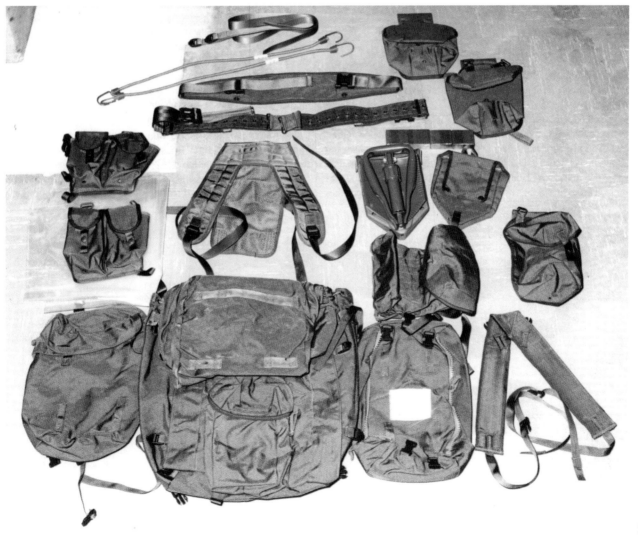

that the male quick-release plastic buckle attachment for the bayonet scabbard is sewn to the side of the right pouch. Eventually, a separate bayonet frog was produced for the set so it could be attached (left or right). The left/ right ammunition pouch concept was carried through into the 1990 set.

Equipment Pouch (Utility)

The trial equipment utility pouch is of a single compartment design and can be worn in place of an ammunition pouch. The yoke attachments are fixed – in this example a left-hand version – with angled loops similar to the ammunition pouch. On the rear, belt loops and a 'C' clip are fitted.

(**Above**) A 58 pattern left-hand ammunition pouch alongside a left-hand PLCE trial pouch. Note the difference in size, the new PLCE item being designed for SA80 30-round magazines. The angled yoke loops on the PLCE pouch would remain on the initial PLCE issue in 1990.

(**Right**) The S10 respirator and desert NBC equipment. The S10 haversack was based on the Mark 2A S6 version but produced in Cordura nylon. Other items include NBC smock and trousers (different sizes are available), detector papers, decontamination pads and puffer bottles (Fuller's earth), NBC suit repair patches and a *Survive to Fight* training pamphlet (this version dated 1983).

The Nuclear Biological and Chemical (NBC) Threat

The potential deployment of nuclear biological and chemical weapons has been a threat in modern warfare ever since the first atomic bombs were detonated in 1945. This threat intensified during the 'cold war', and personal protection equipment to survive such a conflict, more importantly to continue fighting in one, has been developed and issued to soldiers.

The modern NBC suit is effectively a barrier to the chemical agents and radioactive particle material that may be present in the atmosphere. It comes in two halves – smock and trousers are issued in different sizes – and will last on average twenty-four hours. It is worn over combat clothing and boots. Webbing is worn over the top of the NBC suit. The suit is lined with activated charcoal material, and is designed to allow the soldier to operate once the initial (nuclear) deployment has subsided and it is safe to emerge from protective cover.

NBC 'environments' are graded according to the perceived threat or actual conditions, NBC 'Black' being the highest classification. Using training pamphlets and regular exercises, soldiers learn techniques (or drills) for how to eat, drink or go to the toilet whilst wearing suits and respirators, so when they have to be used in combat, the actions are second nature. These drills may need to be conducted while out in the open or within a shelter or vehicle.

The correct identification of the dispersed agent or gas is very important, as not only will a variety of agents be encountered, but different operational techniques for decontamination are required. To assist this, comprehensive NBC testing kits and packs of coloured identification or books of detector papers are issued. The detector papers are attached to the NBC suit at set

locations and usually change a distinctive colour once droplets of the liquid or vapour hit them.

To decontaminate equipment, sachets and bottles are used to dispense Fuller's earth powder; this in turn soaks up the agent, which is then neutralized/ removed from the equipment. All items in contact with the agents must then be decontaminated themselves – including the decontamination devices.

A respirator (more commonly, but incorrectly referred to as a gas mask) is worn to prevent any inhalation of airborne material.

When worn, breathing takes extra effort as the external air is filtered through a special canister to remove the chemical particles. The canister may only last for a few hours depending on the contaminated environment, and then it needs to be changed. Rubber gloves with cloth inners and rubber overboots are issued to protect the hands and feet. Needless to say, it can be a sweaty experience for a soldier wearing a full NBC suit, respirator and carrying a full load of kit. All the NBC equipment must be carried within the modern webbing set, with provision given to its entire storage, quick access and operation.

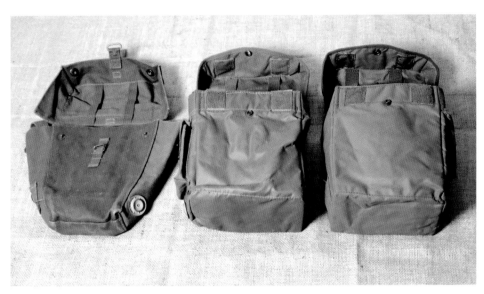

(left) The respirator haversacks issued with the 1958 pattern set in chronological order: left to right: Mark 1, manufactured in cloth material, Mark 2 made in butyl nylon to ease decontamination, and on the right, the Mark 2A also made in butyl nylon. The designs of the haversack were similar, with internal pockets for spare filters, decontamination pads, nerve agent combipens and the anti-dimming device. Externally the haversacks had a strap for carrying across the chest and a pocket for a Fuller's earth puffer bottle (DKP2).

(Below) The S6 respirator and Mark 1 haversack, dated 1965. The other items are a booklet of detector papers and a green tube of anti-dimming paste.

Personal Load-Carrying Equipment (PLCE)

The Personal Load-Carrying Equipment issued in 1990 was the result of many years' research into providing a set of modular flexible load-carrying equipment suitable for the decontamination demands of modern nuclear, biological and chemical warfare. The equipment first saw action in the Balkans conflict and the first Gulf War. It uses the latest materials with a tough Cordura double-layer nylon, and for the first time in equipment manufacture, plastics were used in its construction. Compared to previous patterns, few components were actually metal, such fixings being replaced by modern 'ladder-lock' plastic buckles and 'Spanish' quick-release attachments. The new modular design was completely different from the earlier patterns, allowing soldiers to attach pouches virtually anywhere on the belt, and for the first time a large rucksack suitable for battle loads was issued.

The equipment was initially issued in olive drab, and this was changed to disruptive pattern material (DPM) camouflage from about 1992. Improvements were also made to the pouch-belt attachment methods and pouch closures based on field use. Some olive components continued to be manufactured for some time after the introduction of DPM equipment.

Recent conflicts in Iraq and Afghanistan have finally seen the issue of desert DPM equipment, with items illustrated later in this book.

The olive PLCE equipment featured in this section dates mainly from 1990–91, and depicts the typical items that would have been issued to soldiers during the Iraq/ Gulf War.

The PLCE design (or concept) has also been adopted by other armies, changing the DPM British camouflage pattern for their own type (for example, the German Army using it in a 'Flecktarn' pattern) and modifying the equipment for individual requirements or weapons.

(Below) A Royal Marine takes aim with his 5.56mm (0.223in) L86A1 light support weapon (LSW) during the Gulf War (February 1991). He is wearing the olive-green PLCE equipment with a trial 'snap'-closure utility pouch immediately above the twin ammunition pouches. The olive-green PLCE equipment contrasted badly against the lighter desert environment and was in time often 'camouflaged' with paint. (© Crown Copyright/MoD and Trustees of the Royal Marines Museum)

Background and Overview

Despite the adoption of the smaller SA80/ L85A1 rifle, the average soldier could only fit five standard-sized pouches and the bayonet frog on to the waist belt, which limited space for personal equipment. Soldiers soon found several issues with the early equipment. Prior to PLCE, the 1958 pattern set (with its limitations) afforded reasonable space for a soldier's kit. The point in question can be seen in the illustration, where the equivalent space between equipments is now limited to a single PLCE utility pouch.

Whilst offering a high range of flexibility, the lack of space for personal gear was apparently deliberate (particularly for mechanized roles) to prevent troops overloading themselves with unnecessary items, so they carried only the essentials for twenty-four hours.

The modular functionality of PLCE, having six yoke fittings and a 'left/ right' ammunition pouch arrangement, dictated the positioning of key components. If the soldier wished to fit the respirator pouch or the entrenching tool, then one or two other pouches would have to be sacrificed to accommodate it.

The 'C' clips and Velcro/ Lift the Dot belt-pouch attachments when placed under weight, often came away from the belt and these were changed for tags that slid into the pockets within the length of the belt. The tags were initially metal, but were changed to plastic for DPM kit issue. This also improved comfort when wearing the belt, although a hip pad was issued to attach to the belt's inside surface (often called a 'hippo pad' due to its shape). Slippage with the belt buckle resulted in some soldiers exchanging it unofficially for a metal roll-pin belt.

When a complete set was worn, the equipment tended to be bulky, which posed difficulties, especially within vehicles. The equipment sat lower than 1958 pattern and it pressed uncomfortably on the lower back when the wearer was trying to sit, say within an armoured vehicle.

Other issues affected the materials in early sets. The nylon belt was too stiff (until broken in), and the large plastic Fastex (or side release) buckle tended to occasionally spring open under extreme loads, although this was quickly rectified with a wider, improved and more robust buckle.

(Above) Ladder lock buckles. The use of plastic on webbing items was a new concept, and viewed with some suspicion regarding its longevity. As modern materials have improved, they have become more durable. These buckles (and Fastex clips, similar to the two-prong belt-buckle version) are used throughout the equipment for strap adjustment and fastenings.

(Below) Space for personal kit is at a premium with PLCE, as this comparison between 1958 pattern kidney pouches (top) and PLCE utility pouch (bottom) can be seen. This was apparently deliberate, to ensure soldiers only carried essential equipment on their webbing belt order.

31

(Left) A left-hand trial PLCE ammunition pouch alongside a twin 'SAS' ammunition pouch. It is the opinion of the author that the trial pouch design may have been influenced by this item. Note the popper and Velcro fasteners. Whilst effective, they were initially criticised as being awkward to close and noisy in tactical environments.

The 'Spanish' QRF tabs employed to fix the pouch lids, while effective, sat lightly in their retainers, and any upward movement of the pouch (for example, climbing downwards) tended inadvertently to release them, which could cause items to be lost. The use of a Velcro fastener in conjunction with the tab partly rectified the problem but was noisy when released and not foolproof, especially in the case of the respirator pouch (most exposed from the belt when worn). The alternative solution for the quick-release fasteners was to trap the opening tab downwards into the fastener, then close it shut. However, this had the disadvantage of making the quick-release features slower to open.

The main breakthrough with PLCE was the advantage of repositioning the modular component pouches wherever the sol-dier desired, including swapping an ammunition pouch for a utility pouch. This allowed certain personnel (including medical staff) a degree of flexibility within the set.

Main Components

Waist Belt

The PLCE webbing belt is manufactured from nylon and is sized from small to extra large. It has a series of loops on the inside face, similar to the 1937, 1944 and 1958 patterns, except these are now dual purpose with the pockets accommodating both 'C' clips and attachment tabs (as seen on the new equipment pouches). The belt is adjustable using a length of nylon strapping positioned on

(Left) (Left) Trial PLCE ammunition pouch. (Right) 1990 dated left-hand ammunition pouch. The later design has 'Spanish' quick-release closures and covers fitted to the Velcro, addressing the issues encountered during the trial phase.

the right-hand side. It is fastened with a large 60mm plastic ITW Nexus (Fastex) buckle. To release, the two prongs are depressed and the buckle comes apart. The belt is often used with a hip pad to prevent chafing – a problem encountered with the early 'C' clips, similar to the 1958 pattern. Two metal loops are fitted at the centre rear – these are for the lower back yoke straps/ fittings.

Ammunition Pouch

The 1990 pattern PLCE pouches were initially issued as a left and right set. Each accommodated four 30-round SA80 magazines in two compartments. The compartments were divided into two sections, one for each magazine to prevent rattling. Each pouch was fitted with a 'Spanish' closure, the quick-release (QRF) fittings adopted from Spanish webbing, and these are a modernized version of the QRF first provided in 1944–45 in the 1937/ 1944 pattern equipment sets.

The pouches also have Velcro closures that can be covered or exposed to allow a temporary closure of the pouch (when rapid removal/ reposition of the magazines are needed). This feature is fitted to most of the equipment pouches and addressed the noise problem encountered before.

(Above) (Top) Trial waist belt. (Bottom) 1992 dated PLCE waist belt. Note the larger closure buckle (produced by ITW Nexus) and the adjustment strap.

(Right) The 'Spanish' closures had a tendency to come open if the clip were brushed against a fixed object, so soldiers inserted the pull tab into the loop, locking the fastener loop. This solved the problem, but made the pouch harder to open. Both options are illustrated.

(Below) 1990 Pattern yoke with reversed ammunition pouch to show yoke attachment methods and side straps.

(Below) (Left) Rucksack side pouch yoke; (right) main yoke for the webbing. Note the difference in adjustment/ waist belt strapping and buckles for the side pouches fitted near the Y. For manufacturing simplicity, the chassis of the yokes were the same, with different fittings added.

Bayonet, Scabbard and Bayonet Frog

On PLCE trial equipment the bayonet frog/ scabbard was a fixed attachment to the right-hand pouch. A separate bayonet frog was adopted for the 1990 pattern with provision for two belt positions, high and low fitting. The frog can be removed from the set and the bayonet stored if not required for a particular role. A male

(Above) 1990 PLCE bayonet frog. The Fastex clip for the bayonet scabbard (at left) is folded out of view. Both high/ low belt fittings are provided. Note the markings on the scabbard.

(Below) SA80 bayonet (a later example) with the infantry and 'other arms' scabbards. The

infantry version is fitted with a saw, sharpening stone and wire-cutting boss. The 'other arms' scabbard is plain. Both have a female Fastex clip at the top – this engages into the male clip of the bayonet frog. The bayonet has a hollow handle that fits over the SA80 muzzle. Rounds are fired through this fitting.

Fastex buckle is attached to the top of the webbing frog; this engages into the female clasp on the plastic bayonet scabbard.

The bayonet for the SA80 (L85A1) has been designed to act as a field knife, too. Early-issue versions had a weak attachment clip and it was not unheard of for the bayonet to be launched off the rifle during live firing sessions! It cannot be attached when the blank firing device (BFA) is attached to the rifle; neither can it be attached to the L98 cadet version of the rifle for safety reasons.

Two types of bayonet scabbard are currently issued. An infantry version for front line troops has a saw, wire-cutter lug and a sharpening stone built into the scabbard. The 'other arms' version is a plain scabbard, and the extra fittings are not provided (simply removed). Near the tip of the bayonet, an 'eye' hole is punched through; this marries up with the lug on the scabbard to form wire cutters, the top of the bayonet cutting through the wire when trapped against the metal scabbard recess.

PLCE Rucksack (Bergen)

The design of the original PLCE rucksack (sometimes called a Bergen) can be traced back to the various civilian and military versions used in the Falklands war. Provision of a rucksack to carry heavy loads in reasonable comfort over long distances and to enable troops to be self-sufficient for several weeks on end was a priority.

The PLCE rucksack has a capacity of 100ltr (22gal) in the main compartment, with two extra 10ltr (2.2gal) side pouches. It comes in two versions, a short and long back. The carrying position on the back is typically higher than a normal civilian rucksack, lifting the base above the rear belt webbing pouches and the top is pushed above the wearer's head, so that the rucksack maximizes load capacity and does not foul the belt order arrangement.

Inside, the main single compartment is enclosed with a drawstring rain/ snow cover. There is no dividing compartment, just a full-length sleeve running down the rear to accept the aluminium internal frame (either a two- or three-leg 'prong' type). The lid has zipped pockets to both internal and external surfaces.

On both sides of the rucksack, the side pouches can be attached/ detached using large plastic zips. The side pockets can be zipped together independently of the rucksack and used in conjunction with a side pouch yoke to make a 20ltr (4.4gal) 'day-sack' or patrol sack. The side zips are of a universal design so that other items such as medical kits or two rifle grenade carriers can be attached in place of the pouches. The side pouches can also be attached to the rucksack using four Fastex clips (two at the top and

(Below) Inside the lid. Note the zipped pocket. The equipment label can be seen in the centre. This is a long-backed rucksack produced in 1991. The contents are protected from the elements with a drawstring cover. There is a full-length internal frame housed in its own compartment.

(Top right) The PLCE rucksack was based on civilian designs and adopted many useful features, the main one being detachable side pouches. This example has one side

pouch attached to its right-hand side. Note the small pocket at the base (for engineer/ radio equipment), adjustable straps and fixing points on the lid and surfaces. A zipped pocket is provided on the lid for small items.

(Right) The PLCE rucksack view to the back, showing the grab handle, adjustable shoulder straps and waist belt. An identification patch is provided in the centre. This version belongs to the author and has accompanied him on many exercises!

two at the bottom of the rucksack). The Fastex clips are compatible with the fittings on ammunition and utility pouches, so that if needed other items from the set can be attached to the rucksack. Usually the side pouches remain fixed using both the buckles and zips.

On both sides of the rucksack (under the side pockets, visible when removed) are three horizontal adjustable straps/ buckles. These allow the vertical attachment of longer items, for example a rolled sleeping mat or perhaps skis. On the front of the rucksack a small zipped pouch is provided. Whatever the intended purpose of this pouch, possibly a personal radio, it is typically the home of a spare 1958 water bottle and the soldier's brew kit!

If additional kit is necessary, it can be strapped on externally using the two PLCE utility straps or spare rubber bungee cords to the sack. Additional anchorage points are provided on the lid and sides to facilitate this.

On the rear surface (against the back), two adjustable shoulder straps, a large grab handle, identification patch and waist belt are attached. The waist belt is not normally worn with the webbing and is folded back as it can prevent quick removal of the rucksack if needed. The padded shoulder straps can also be adjusted for length and tension, to support varying loads.

Three waterproof draw-cord liners are provided with the rucksack, one large item for the main compartment liner and two small bags for the individual side pouches, although these are usually used elsewhere.

In summary, the PLCE rucksack is a well thought out item and certainly superior to the 1958-pattern large pack it replaced. The disadvantage of having 120ltr (26gal) of space on hand is that soldiers tend to fill it up!

(Top left) View of the side pouch attached to the rucksack.

(Left) Side pouch removed, revealing the strapping and zip detail. The straps can be used to lash sleeping mats or other long items against the sack.

(Above) Rear view of rucksack side pouches making up the patrol or day sack. Both are connected using zips that run along the trailing edges.

Rucksack Side Pouches

The two side pouches (each 10ltr/ 2.2gal capacity) attach to the rucksack using plastic zips and Fastex buckles as described above. Each pouch is a single compartment item (in 1990 pattern) with a zip/ covered lid. These are detachable and can be zipped together (off the rucksack) to form a small patrol sack and are carried on a unique yoke (as in the illustration). The pouches are also fitted with external loops to allow extra kit to be strapped to them using utility straps.

More recent developments of the side pouches include provision of an internal sleeve for water bladders, or designs produced for section medical kits.

In practice, a side pouch is usually dedicated to NBC equipment and marked accordingly by the soldier. To prevent loss, early pouches have a white name label at the rear; this changed to a matt green nylon patch from 1989/90 onwards.

Yoke – Side Pouches

The yoke issued for attaching the rucksack's side pockets, either one centrally or two zipped together to make a patrol or day sack, is different from the main yoke issued for the belt order. The basic mesh panel is the same to both items; however, the side yoke is produced with additional buckles fixed to the shoulder arms, for clipping on the pouches (top) and buckles fixed at the bottom to secure the base of the side pockets. A thin waist belt is fixed at the base, although in practice this is often used as a supplementary strap tied around the pouches. The shoulder straps have adjustable fixings, and Fastex clip(s) are used to fix to the trailing edge of the pouches when two are worn side by side. The side-pouch yoke is usually carried rolled up in the rucksack lid pocket for convenience.

(Below) Rucksack side pouches attached to the yoke, as worn next to the back. Alternatively the waist belt can be connected around the pouches if desired.

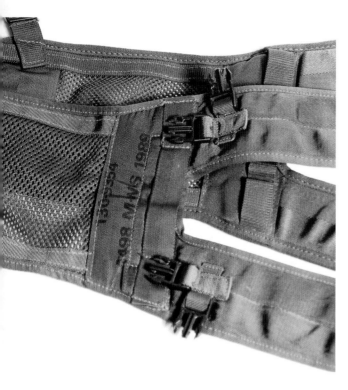

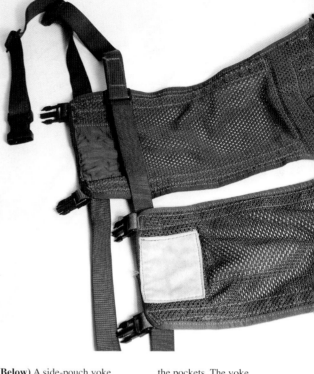

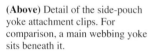

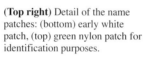

(Above) Detail of the side-pouch yoke attachment clips. For comparison, a main webbing yoke sits beneath it.

(Top right) Detail of the name patches: (bottom) early white patch, (top) green nylon patch for identification purposes.

(Below) A side-pouch yoke showing waist belt and adjustable straps that connect to the base of the pockets. The yoke accommodates either a single side pouch, or both zipped together.

Utility Straps

Two long utility straps are issued with the set to enable extra kit to be fixed to the side pouches, rucksack or the belt order as required.

PLCE Order Configurations

The most common configurations of PLCE are:

- Assault order: belt kit with a single side pouch attached to the yoke – for short patrols only.
- Combat/ patrol order: as above, with NBC kit and twenty-four hours' food supply. Either side pouches or a small patrol rucksack are attached.
- Marching order: belt kit, and a rucksack for long duration patrol.

(Above) Two utility straps are provided with the set to attach extra kit. Note the plastic buckle.

(Below) PLCE belt kit: items left to right – waist belt, (left) twin ammunition pouch, utility pouch, entrenching tool/ cover, water-bottle pouch; and (right) twin ammunition pouch. The yoke (above) spreads the weight of the equipment over the shoulders.

(Above) (Above) the SA80 sling, and (below) the nylon SLR sling. The new weapon sling allowed the rifle to be carried in a variety of positions against the body. The item on the right is a protective cover for the SUSAT sight.

(Below) The SA80 cleaning kit (roll) and contents is shown both open and rolled up. Items in the kit include barrel/ chamber brushes, cleaning rods/ T Bar, oil bottle, 4 × 2 cleaning patches and a pull-through. The green tube is a muzzle cover.

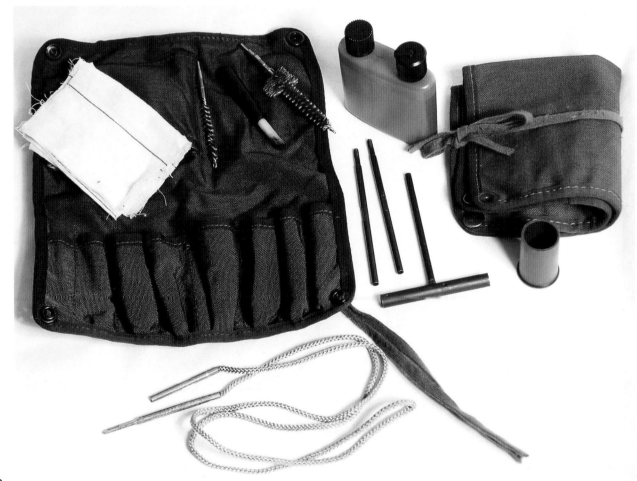

Ancillary Items

The following are other related items worthy of note to collectors.

SA80 Sling and Cleaning Kit

Produced in PLCE nylon webbing, the SA80 sling allows a variety of options for wearing the SA80, including vertically down the back. The rifle can quickly be dropped from the usual 'high port' position into the aim position by releasing the Fastex clip. The cleaning kits issued with the L85A1 were provided in a nylon cover. Collectors may wish to acquire such a kit, as it is an interesting addition to 1990–91-dated PLCE equipment sets.

Pack Medical Equipment

The 'pack medical equipment' consists of three compartments and can be carried on the PLCE belt using a belt loop. It has three compartments: the two smaller sections are filled with shell dressings, and the larger section contains medical equipment to treat trauma injuries. These packs are usually available with the medical contents in place, and finding one that is intact will appeal to collectors.

Rifle Grenade Pouch

Before the underslung grenade launcher (similar to the US M203 system), an SA80 rifle grenade was issued. Spare grenades were

(Above) Left: olive version of the rifle grenade pouch with fully contained tubes and (right) the 'open' DPM version. Rifle grenades have been replaced by the underslung grenade launcher (UGL), a system similar to the US M203.

(Right) The medical pack closed. Note the Fastex closure and strap. The pack is fixed to the belt with a simple belt loop.

(Below) The three-section 'pack medical equipment' shown open. The two lower compartments contain field dressings.

carried in this item – both the olive and DPM items are illustrated here. Zips are provided to the sides allowing two pouches to be connected (four grenades in total) and placed on to a rucksack (in lieu of the side pouch), or a strap can be fixed to the rear of the carrier to allow it to be carried on the shoulder or attached to the rear of belt equipment.

PLCE Improvements

The original olive-green PLCE saw extensive use during the Gulf War; this highlighted several minor problems with the pattern, which were soon rectified. A number of changes were introduced from 1991, namely an improvement to the pouch-belt attachment

(Above) The universal ammunition pouch was produced from 1991 and superseded the left/ right ammunition pouch set. Not all troops were issued with two ammunition pouches: some units issued a utility pouch in lieu of an ammunition pouch, which was worn at the front of the set. This example has one Velcro patch exposed, the other

covered. The pouch could now be closed quickly, for example when under attack.

(Above right) The rear of the 1991 universal ammunition pouch showing belt tabs and a separate 'A' clip for illustration.

(Below) The inside surface of the PLCE belt, showing pockets. During 1991, the belt fixings were revised to include attachment tabs, which slot into pockets provided on the PLCE belt. The Velcro tab and popper then make this a secure, and also a flexible fitting, as the pouch can be removed from the set without having to disassemble the belt kit if

necessary. This DPM utility pouch now has a single set of such fixings and a set of belt loops (hidden under the belt). The lower strips of loops are used to thread cord around in order to eliminate pouch 'bounce' when running. The 1990 utility pouch (olive) version previously had two rows (a lower set). The metal loops on top of the belt are for the rear yoke straps.

(Right) The rear of the pouches showing the fixing methods. Top left: trial left ammunition pouch (1985), (bottom left) PLCE left ammunition pouch, (top right) universal ammunition pouch with 'tab' belt fixings and 'A' clips at the top of the pouch (1991). Bottom right: DPM camouflage pouch (1992).

(Right) Front view of the PLCE pouches. Top left: trial left ammunition pouch with popper closures; bottom left, PLCE left ammunition pouch with 'Spanish' closures; (top right) universal ammunition pouch. Bottom right: DPM camouflage ammunition pouch.

prone to coming undone. The Osprey and LCTV pouches are labelled differently, with examples seen by the author including the utility and medical pouches. These are identical in design and share the same NSN; in the case of the medical pouch it is 8465-99-480-8051.

The range of standard LCTV pouches includes: utility (general purpose) (3), small utility (1), water bottle (1), medical (1), knife/ torch (1), 40mm grenade (2), SA80A2 ammunition (2), anti-personnel grenade (2) and a MK6A helmet bag (1).

(Right) Detail of the internal zipped pouch – notebooks, maps or a pistol can be inserted into the loops/ fixings as indicated.

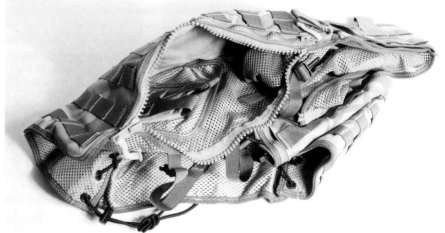

(Right) Wider view of the internal pocket. There is another small pouch provided at the rear of the jacket.

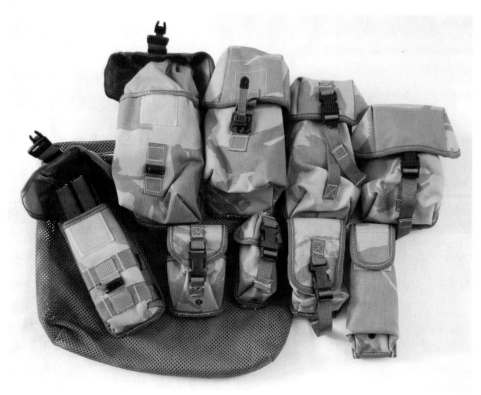

(Left) Pouches provided for the load-carrying tactical vest include (clockwise): SA80 A2 ammunition (2), utility pouch (3) with internal sand cover, water bottle pouch (1), small utility pouch (1), medical pouch (1) with panel for marking blood group of wearer, knife/ torch pouch (1), helmet bag pouch (1), 40mm grenade pouch (2), anti-personnel grenade pouch (2) and a helmet bag (1). The method of attachment is the same as the Osprey series. Other pouches provided with the Osprey system include pistol holster, drop leg harness, armoured brassards, full and half protective collars. Recognizing that desert environments are invariably hot and people can get dehydrated quickly, water-carrying bladders (commonly called Camelbaks after their manufacturer) have been designed into the set and PLCE equipment, to attach to the rear four Fastex clips on the LCTV.

56

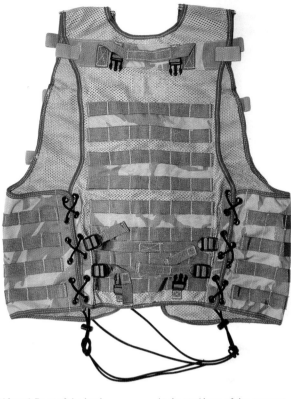

(**Above**) Pouches attached to the load-carrying tactical vest, showing the flexibility of the attachments. Although the manufacturers suggest a layout, the position of the pouches can be altered to suit user preference.

(**Above**) Rear of the load-carrying tactical vest. If the rucksack is not worn, extra items can be fixed to the PALS fixings. At the top/ base of the garment, Fastex clips are provided for attaching a rucksack side pouch or a Camelbak water bladder.

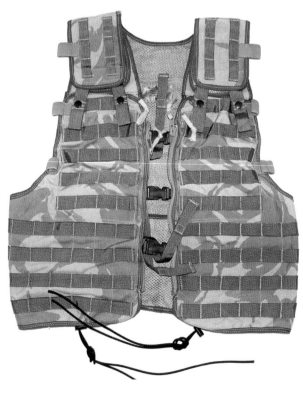

(**Above**) Detail of the PALS/ MOLLE fixings. The straps fix on to the poppers exposed at the base of the pouch.

(**Right**) Load-carrying tactical vest (LCTV), front view. The vest is closed using three Fastex clips. The black shock cords are for adjusting the vest to the user.

57

(Above) Royal Marines in Afghanistan with Osprey body armour pose for the camera adjacent to a Viking tracked vehicle. Note the SA80 bayonet, magazine speed-loading clip and small Maglite torch tucked into the MOLLE straps. Osprey pouches include a small utility and a helmet pouch. The leg-harness and (side) pouches appear to be of commercial or self-purchase origin. (© Trustees of the Royal Marines Museum)

(Left) Front of Mark Two Osprey equipment fitted with protective collar and arm/ shoulder brassards.

Effectiveness

Body armour equipment is a trade-off between protection and mobility. Too much weight and the soldier is unable to operate for long periods or worse, is unable to move at all! Carrying full body armour, webbing and a rucksack in a hot terrain is not conducive to long-term mobility, so in the case of Osprey or Kestrel body armour, the protection afforded is restricted to the major organs; the extremities – arms/ legs – are partially uncovered (although extension protection can be fitted). A hit in these areas (although painful and incapacitating) is unlikely to be fatal. When the armour plate is hit, the wearer gets the full shock impact of the plate across the body, as the bullet's energy is arrested by absorbing the impact across the plate. This will most certainly bruise the soldier in due course, but this is clearly a better outcome than an unopposed high velocity rifle bullet striking the body.

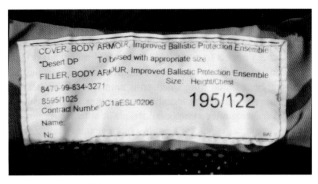

(**Above**) Label as inserted in the Kestrel body-armour jacket.

(**Right**) Front view of the Kestrel body-armour jacket. Note the central pocket for the enhanced armour plate, the flared collar, and strips for the lateral adjustment straps (not shown). A Mark 2 version with PALS / MOLLE fittings and larger plates was issued, but Kestrel is now usually superseded in theatre by Osprey vests.

(**Right**) Rear view of the Kestrel body-armour jacket, with pouch for enhanced armour plate.

Further Reading

I trust that this exploration into modern British webbing equipment and concepts has been informative and will enable the reader to expand a collection. Below is a list of related books, museums and websites that you may find useful for research and general militaria interest.

    Any contact with the author can be made in the first instance via the publisher. Details can be found within the front cover.

Related Books

Chappell, M. *British Infantry Equipments (2) 1908–2000* (Osprey) ISBN 1-85532-839-9.

Chappell, M. *The British Soldier in the 20th Century, Part 3 – Personal Equipment 1945 to the present day* (Wessex Military Publishing) ISBN 1-870498-02-X.

Howlett, S. *British Post-War Jungle Webbing* (The Crowood Press) ISBN 978-1-84797-086-2.

Lane, M. *Items of British Web Equipment, 1937–2002* (Galago Publishing Ltd) ISBN 978-0946995691.

Places of Interest

Royal Marines Museum (www.royalmarinesmuseum.co.uk)

Imperial War Museum (www.iwm.org.uk)

D-Day Museum (www.ddaymuseum.co.uk)

Useful Websites

Britain's Small Wars (www.britains-smallwars.com)

Falklands Museum (www.falklands1982.com)

Historic news reports
(www.itnsource.com or www.britishpathe.com)

British Army (www.army.mod.uk)